Chinese Australians

Book 5

The Chinese Legacy

How Migration, Culture and Community have Influenced Australia

Marji Hill

Published by The Prison Tree Press 2025

Copyright © 2025 Marji Hill

The Prison Tree Press
Suite 124
1-10 Albert Avenue
Broadbeach, Queensland 4218
https://marjihill.com

ISBN 9781764339209 Hardback
ISBN 9781764339216 eBook

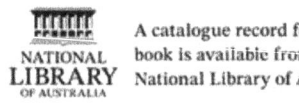 A catalogue record for this book is available from the National Library of Australia

All rights reserved. No part of this book may be reproduced, stored in a retrieval system, or transmitted in any form or by any means, electronic, mechanical, photocopying, recording, scanning, or otherwise, without the prior written permission of the publisher.

Disclaimer:

All the material contained in this book is provided for educational and informational purposes only. No responsibility can be taken for any results or outcomes resulting from the use of this material.

While every care has been taken to trace and acknowledge copyright the publishers tender their apologies for any accidental infringement where copyright has proved untraceable.

Every attempt has been made to provide information that is both accurate and effective, however, the author does not assume any responsibility for the accuracy or use/misuse of this information.

Acknowledgement is given to Canva for most of the illustrations in this book. The paintings, however, were created by Marji Hill.

THE SERIES

Chinese Australians

Book 1

Australia and China

Before Captain Cook

Book 2

Early Chinese Migrants

The First Chinese Australians

Book 3

Chinese and Gold

The Chinese on the Australian Goldfields

Book 4

The Chinese Experience

The Untold Story of Prejudice and Violence on the Australian Goldfields

Book 5

The Chinese Legacy

How Migration, Culture and Community have Influenced Australia

Acknowledgements

I acknowledge the Traditional Custodians
of Country throughout Australia
and their connections to land, sea, and community.

I pay my respect to elders, past, present, and emerging
and extend my respect to all First Nations peoples today.
In the spirit of reconciliation,
my mission is to increase understanding
between the First Nations and other Australians
and to provide people from all over the globe
some basic understanding of Australia s first people,
their history, and cultures.

In addition,
I thank Eddie Dowd for helping me get this book
into its final form for publication.
I also acknowledge the support
from John and Sherien Foley.

Marji Hill

Table of Contents

1.	Chinatown	1
2.	Why Did Chinese People Come to Australia?	5
3.	Life on the Goldfields	7
4.	Facing Discrimination	9
5.	Building Communities	11
6.	Chinese Contributions to Australian Life	13
7.	Business, Trade and Economy	15
8.	Language	19
9.	Celebrations	21
10.	Education and Exchange	23
11.	A New Wave of Migration	25
12.	The Future Relationship Between China and Australia	27
13.	Celebrating Diversity	29

GLOSSARY:	31
SOURCES	33
ABOUT MARJI HILL	35
MORE BOOKS BY MARJI HILL	37

1. Chinatown

Picture this: you are walking through a busy street in Sydney's Chinatown. Dixon Street is its main street. There are many shops and Chinese restaurants. At the entrance are ceremonial Chinese archways and red lanterns hang above gently swaying in the wind.

Ceremonial archway

In this car-free street there are lots of mouth-watering restaurants hidden within the narrow cobblestone laneways. There are different types of

Chinese food, from dim sims to Szechuan spicy dishes. Enjoy Yum Cha and the different array of foods which are offered on steaming trolleys around the restaurants. The smell of dumplings and noodles fills the air.

Enjoy Yum Cha and the different array of foods

People are laughing, shopping, and eating together. You can find everything there, from small specialist stores and Asian grocers to noodle bars in hidden food halls and tucked-away fine-dining restaurants.

You hear different voices speaking English, Mandarin and Cantonese.

You might even spot a lion dance performance during the Chinese New Year festival. This is a great time in Chinatown which buzzes with energy and vibrancy.

Sydney, Melbourne, and Adelaide have very prominent Chinatowns. Other cities like Brisbane and Perth also have Chinatowns, reflecting the long-standing presence of Chinese communities in Australia.

Chinatowns in Australia are places where Chinese culture is celebrated. They are also a sign of how much the Chinese community has shaped Australia since the 1800s. From early migrants to today's students, businesspeople and families, Chinese Australians have helped build the country we live in now.

Chinese New Year

2. Why Did Chinese People Come to Australia?

In the early 1800s, life in China was very hard. Many families were poor, and there were floods, famines, and not enough work. Food was often scarce, especially in the countryside.

At the same time, the population was growing quickly, so there was even more pressure on land and resources. Armed gangs sometimes attacked villages, stealing food and forcing people off their land.

In the early 1800s, life in China was very hard

Then, in the 1850s, amazing news spread across the world — gold had been discovered in Australia!

People from many countries rushed to the goldfields of Victoria, in places like Ballarat and Bendigo, hoping to make their fortune. Thousands of Chinese men joined this rush. Most came from the southern part of China.

Life in China was crowded, and the government in the big cities did little to help rural families. Young men were encouraged to leave China and work in Australia. These men had to repay their travel costs from their wages once they arrived.

Only men were allowed to migrate. Wives and children were not allowed to come. Families had to stay behind in China, often helping to pay off debts if needed.

The journey to Australia was long and dangerous. Migrants travelled by ship in crowded conditions, taking weeks to cross the ocean. Some even landed in South Australia and walked hundreds of kilometres to the Victorian goldfields. They did this to avoid a special tax that was unfairly charged only to Chinese miners.

These Chinese migrants were brave. They left behind hardship and uncertainty, hoping to find gold, earn money and build a better life in Australia.

3. Life on the Goldfields

Life on the goldfields was crowded, noisy, and tough. Most miners lived in tents or simple huts. The work was difficult, and the weather could be very hot or freezing cold.

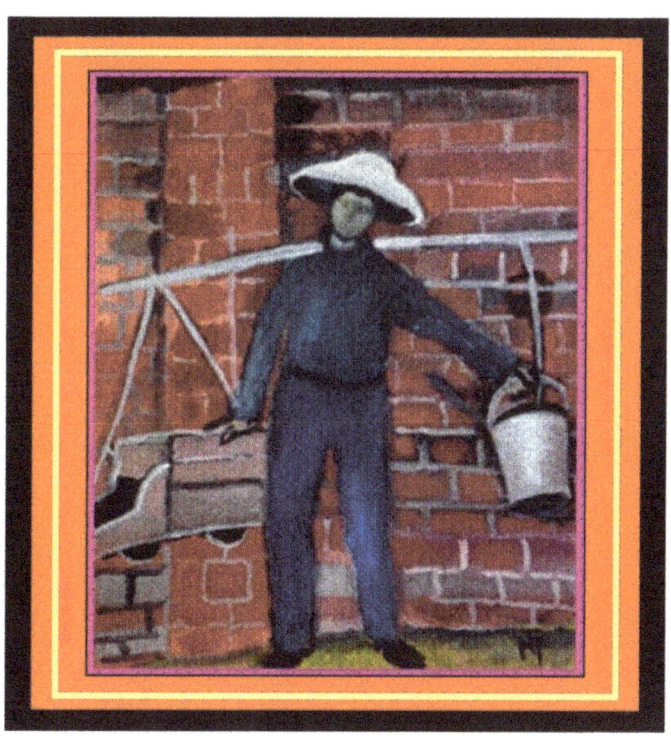

Chinese gold miner

Chinese miners usually worked together in teams. They shared their gold and looked after each other. They were known for being patient, organised, and very hard-working. If other miners had already searched an area, the Chinese miners would carefully rework the claims and still find gold that had been missed.

But life was not just about finding gold. Many Chinese migrants started small businesses like food stalls, shops and laundries. They helped build the towns around the goldfields. Others created market gardens, growing fresh vegetables to sell to the local people. Their knowledge of farming helped turn dry land into healthy gardens.

The Chinese created market gardens

4. Facing Discrimination

The Chinese were not always treated fairly.

Some European miners did not like the Chinese way of working or the fact that they were successful. These miners started to blame the Chinese for their own problems.

As a result, many Chinese people faced discrimination, prejudice and violence. There were even riots where Chinese miners were attacked. Laws were made to make life harder for Chinese migrants. For example, there were special taxes just for Chinese people.

Later, in 1901, the Australian Government passed the "White Australia Policy". This law made it very hard for non-Europeans to enter the country. It meant that very few Chinese people were allowed to migrate to Australia for many decades.

5. Building Communities

Even during tough times, Chinese Australians continued to build strong communities. They set up temples, schools and shops. Chinatowns began to appear in cities like Melbourne, Sydney and Brisbane.

These areas became centres of Chinese culture and life.

People helped each other find work, places to live, and ways to celebrate their traditions. They formed groups and clubs, ran newspapers in Chinese and organised cultural events.

Chinese temple

During times of hardship, these communities offered support and friendship. And today, they are still important meeting places for Chinese Australians and anyone interested in Chinese culture.

6. Chinese Contributions to Australian Life

When we think about what makes Australia special, it is not just the beaches, bush or outback. It is also the people who live here and the cultures they bring.

The Chinese have had a huge influence on Australia. Chinese Australians have shaped the way we eat, celebrate, work and live together.

What is your favourite takeaway meal? For many Australians, it is Chinese! Dishes like fried rice, sweet and sour pork, dumplings and dim sims are super popular. Ingredients such as soy sauce, ginger, and sesame oil are now found in most Australian kitchens.

Chinese restaurants are everywhere. Friday night dinner often means Chinese food for lots of families.

7. Business, Trade and Economy

When Chinese people first came to Australia, many worked as farmers or market gardeners. They were famous for their hard work. They introduced new crops and smart gardening techniques.

They also worked in industries like furniture making and shopkeeping, some opening small grocery stores. In the cities, others ran laundries, import–export businesses and manufactured furniture. They also helped set up medicine shops and cultural groups.

Over time, these businesses became important parts of local communities.

Chinese herbal medicine

Many Chinese workers built important roads and railways, including the Darwin–Pine Creek railway, which helped towns grow and connect.

Today, Chinese Australians continue to play a big role in business. The Chinatowns in the major cities are busy centres full of shops, markets, and restaurants.

**Senator Penny Wong,
Australian Minister for Foreign Affairs**

On a larger scale, China is one of Australia's most important trading partners selling and buying more goods with China than with any other country. China became Australia's largest trading partner in late 2007 and has remained so since, with two-way trade increasing significantly over the past decades.

With China being their biggest trading partner, Australia exports things like iron ore, natural gas and agricultural products.

Chinese investors have also put money into Australian buildings, roads and other projects. Chinese tourists and students spend money in Australia, helping our shops, hotels and schools. The Australia-China engagement in education, science, business and culture brings significant economic, social and cultural dividends to both countries.

Chinese lanterns

8. Language

Did you know that after English, Mandarin is the most spoken language in Australia? Cantonese is also widely spoken.

Many children grow up speaking both English and Chinese, which keeps their culture strong while also being part of everyday Australian life.

9. Celebrations

One of the most exciting times of the year is Chinese New Year.

Across Australia, cities and towns come alive with fireworks, red lanterns, lion dances, and delicious feasts.

Families give red envelopes with money for good luck, and everyone — no matter their background — is welcome to join the fun.

10. Education and Exchange

Many Chinese people move to Australia for education. Thousands of students come here every year to study at our universities.

Many Chinese people move to Australia for education

They bring fresh ideas, skills, and talents, enriching our classrooms and communities. Some stay on to work as doctors, teachers, or business leaders while others return to China, taking their Australian experiences with them.

From food and farming to festivals and friendships, Chinese Australians have helped shape our country in countless ways. Their contributions make Australia a richer, more colourful and more connected place to live.

11. A New Wave of Migration

In the 1970s when Australia ended the White Australia Policy, people from all over the world could once again migrate to Australia. Chinese migration began to grow again.

The year 1973 was a significant milestone in the history of Chinese Australians. The 'White Australia' Policy was abolished by the Whitlam Government — a victory for the Chinese community.

In 2011, there were well over 300,000 Chinese-born people living in Australia. By 2021 approximately 1.39 million people of Chinese ancestry lived in Australia, which represented about 5.5% of the total population. Today, Chinese-born Australians make up the third largest migrant group in the country, after people from the United Kingdom and India.

Many Chinese were born in Australia and many have come from Mainland China. They have come as students, visitors or workers. Others have come from Hong Kong, Taiwan and Southeast Asia.

Chinese-Australian communities have flourished and contributed to many aspects of Australian life.

12. The Future Relationship Between China and Australia

While China and Australia are very close trading partners and share many cultural links, this close relationship also brings its challenges.

Some worry that the Chinese Government may try to have too much influence in Australia. There are also tensions between China and countries like the United States. Because Australia is a strong ally of the United States, this sometimes creates unease.

Australian Prime Minister Anthony Albanese meeting with Chinese President Xi Jinping

Another concern is about safety and security. Experts warn that spying and cyber-attacks could cause problems. There have also been worries about money given to politicians which could be used to try to influence decisions. Some Chinese-language newspapers and media in Australia are also thought to be influenced by the Chinese Government.

Australia needs to carefully balance its friendships. On one hand, it wants to keep strong ties with China for trade and cultural exchange. On the other hand, it must also protect its democracy, national security and its close alliance with the United States.

These are complicated issues. Australia must work carefully to protect its political structures, freedoms and sovereignty while still respecting its Chinese community and continuing trade.

China's influence in Australia is a complex and evolving issue with both benefits and risks. While Australia benefits from its economic ties with China, there are growing concerns about the potential for political interference, national security threats and the erosion of democratic values.

13. Celebrating Diversity

Despite the challenges, Chinese Australians enrich our nation. From gold miners to modern businesspeople, from farmers to university students, Chinese migrants have played a key role in the Australian story.

Lanterns are part of Chinese festivals and celebrations

Their contributions can be seen in every part of Australian life — from our food and festivals to our economy and communities. As we look to the future, it is important to learn from the past and celebrate the diverse cultures that make Australia such a unique and special place.

By learning about the Chinese-Australian story, we can better understand how migration shapes our country and how everyone — no matter where they come from — can make a difference.

GLOSSARY:

Chinatown — An area where Chinese businesses and cultural activities are located.

Cultural Diversity — A mix of different cultures living together in one place.

Discrimination — Treating someone unfairly because of their race, culture, or background.

Gold Rush — A time when many people came to an area to find gold.

Mandarin — A Chinese language that is widely spoken around the world.

Migration — Moving from one country to another to live.

Trade Partner — A country that buys and sells goods with another country.

White Australia Policy — A law that made it hard for people who were not from Europe to live in Australia.

SOURCES

The author would like to acknowledge the following sources of information:

Grassby, Al & Hill, Marji (2000) *Chinese Australians*. South Yarra, Vic, Macmillan.

Hill, Marji (2022) *Gold and the Chinese: Racism, Riots and Protest on the Australian Goldfields*. Broadbeach, Qld, The Prison Tree Press.

Mo Yimei (1988) "Harvest of endurance: a history of the Chinese in Australia 1788-1988" Sydney, *Australia-China Friendship Society*. http://www.multiculturalaustralia.edu.au/doc/yimei_1.pdf

Ng, David (2024) "Recent Chinese Migration Trends in Australia." *China Source Quarterly*, 11 March.

ABOUT MARJI HILL

Marji Hill runs her art career alongside her career as an author. She is a highly respected international author as well as a seasoned business executive, researcher and coach.

Marji is passionate about promoting understanding between Australia's First Nations people and other Australians. The spirit of reconciliation was fostered in all her writings ever since she was a Research Fellow in Education at the Australian Institute of Aboriginal and Torres Strait Islander Studies (AIATSIS) in Canberra.

From 2008 to 2011, Marji was Deputy Chairperson of the Mosman Branch of Reconciliation Australia in Sydney. Following her Research Fellowship at AIATSIS in 1976 Marji, together with her late partner, Alex Barlow, produced more than seventy (70) books on all aspects of the First Nations people including the critical, annotated bibliography *Black Australia*.

In 1989 she was the Project Coordinator and one of the researchers and writers of *Australian Aboriginal Culture* the official Australian Government publication on First Nations people.

In 1988 *Six Australian Battlefields* was published by Angus and Robertson. A decade later it was re-published by Allen & Unwin as a paperback edition. Her nine-volume encyclopaedia, *Macmillan Encyclopaedia of Australia's Aboriginal Peoples* was published in 2000 and in 2009 she published *The Apology: Saying Sorry To The Stolen Generations*.

Marji's more recent publications extend to self-improvement and self-help with books like *Staying Young Growing Old* and *Inspired by Country* a self-help book about painting with gouache.

MORE BOOKS BY MARJI HILL

First Nations

Hill, Marji 2021 *Australian Aboriginal History: 5 Stories of Indigenous Heroes.* Broadbeach, Qld, The Prison Tree Press.

Hill, Marji 2021 *First People Then and Now: Introducing Indigenous Australians.* 2nd ed. Broadbeach, Qld, The Prison Tree Press.

Aboriginal Global Pioneers

Hill, Marji 2024 *Australian Aboriginal Origins: Earliest Beginnings.* Broadbeach, Qld, The Prison Tree Press. (Book 1)

Hill, Marji 2024 *Australian Aboriginal Trade: Sharing Goods and Services.* Broadbeach, Qld, The Prison Tree Press. (Book 2)

Hill, Marji 2024 *Australian Aboriginal Religion: Country and Dreaming.* Broadbeach, Qld, The Prison Tree Press. (Book 3)

Hill, Marji 2024 *Australian Aboriginal Fire: Managing Country.* Broadbeach, Qld, The Prison Tree Press. (Book 4)

Hill, Marji 2024 *Australian Aboriginal Medicine: Caring for People.* Broadbeach, Qld, The Prison Tree Press. (Book 5)

Self-improvement/Self-Help

Hill, Marji 2014 *Staying Young Growing Old.* Broadbeach, Qld, The Prison Tree Press.

Hill, Marji 2020 *How Big Is Your Why? An Author's Guide to Time Management and Productivity to Achieve Transformational Results.* Broadbeach, Qld, The Prison Tree Press.

Hill, Marji 2020 *A Create and Publish Toolbox: 101 Prompts In A Guided Journal To Help You Write, Self-publish, And Market Your Book on Amazon.* Broadbeach, Qld, The Prison Tree Press.

Hill, Marji 2021 *Inspired by Country: An Artist's Journey Back to Nature, Landscape Painting with Gouache.* Broadbeach, Qld, The Prison Tree Press.

Hill, Marji 2024 *Australian Paintings: Artworks by Marji Hill.* Broadbeach, Qld, The Prison Tree Press.

Gold

Hill, Marji 2022 *Gates of Gold: The Discovery of Gold, its Legacy and its Contribution to Australian Identity.* Broadbeach, Qld, The Prison Tree Press.

Hill, Marji 2022 *Shadows of Gold: Eureka and the Birth of Australian Democracy.* Broadbeach, Qld, The Prison Tree Press.

Hill, Marji 2022 *Gold and the Chinese: Racism, Riots and Protest on the Australian Goldfields.* Broadbeach, Qld, The Prison Tree Press.

Hill, Marji 2022 *Ghosts of Gold: The Life and Times of Jupiter Mosman.* Broadbeach, Qld, The Prison Tree Press.

Hill, Marji 2022 *Blood Gold: Native Police, Bushrangers & Law and Order on the Goldfields.* Broadbeach, Qld, The Prison Tree Press.

www.ingramcontent.com/pod-product-compliance
Lightning Source LLC
Chambersburg PA
CBHW041219240426
43661CB00012B/1085